100+ One-Minute
THOUGHT
Managers

Trilogy Christian Publishers
A Wholly Owned Subsidiary of Trinity Broadcasting Network
2442 Michelle Drive
Tustin, CA 92780

Copyright © 2024 by Dr. Vander Warner, Jr.

Unless otherwise noted, all Scripture quotations are taken from the King James Version of the Bible. Public domain. Scripture quotations marked AMP are taken from the Amplified® Bible (AMP), Copyright © 2015 by The Lockman Foundation. Used by permission. www.lockman.org. Scripture quotations marked ESV are taken from the ESV® Bible (The Holy Bible, English Standard Version®), copyright © 2001 by Crossway Bibles, a publishing ministry of Good News Publishers. Used by permission. All rights reserved. Scripture quotations marked NIV are taken from the Holy Bible, New International Version®, NIV®. Copyright © 1973, 1978, 1984, 2011 by Biblica, Inc.™ Used by permission of Zondervan. All rights reserved worldwide. www.zondervan.com. The "NIV" and "New International Version" are trademarks registered in the United States Patent and Trademark Office by Biblica, Inc.™. Scripture quotations marked NKJV are taken from the New King James Version®. Copyright © 1982 by Thomas Nelson. Used by permission. All rights reserved.

All rights reserved, including the right to reproduce this book or portions thereof in any form whatsoever.
For information, address Trilogy Christian Publishing
Rights Department, 2442 Michelle Drive, Tustin, CA 92780.
Trilogy Christian Publishing/ TBN and colophon are trademarks of Trinity Broadcasting Network.
For information about special discounts for bulk purchases, please contact Trilogy Christian Publishing.
Trilogy Disclaimer: The views and content expressed in this book are those of the author and may not necessarily reflect the views and doctrine of Trilogy Christian Publishing or the Trinity Broadcasting Network.

10 9 8 7 6 5 4 3 2 1
Library of Congress Cataloging-in-Publication Data is available.
ISBN 979-8-89041-969-9
E-ISBN: 979-8-89041-970-5

100+ One-Minute
THOUGHT
Managers

Dr. Vander Warner, Jr.

— ACKNOWLEDGMENTS —

I would like to acknowledge and thank all of the following, without whom this book would have been more difficult to publish: Chuck Smith, my wife, Winnie Warner, and family, Leslie Gilreath Samara, the congregation from the Bible Fellowship at Rockville, and many others whose kind words of encouragement meant more than they know.

TABLE OF CONTENTS

ACKNOWLEDGEMENTS 5

FOREWORD 13

PREFACE 15

GIVE ME THAT OLD-TIME RELIGION 17

WHAT'S DRIVING YOU 18

FAITH AT DAD'S FUNERAL 19

DON'T AGREE WITH CAN'T-ERS 20

THE DEVIL'S BEST TOOL 21

WHEN YOU THINK YOU ARE THROUGH 22

FIND THE KITCHEN 23

LIFE'S MOST INFLUENTIAL VOICE 24

KEEP YOUR PIT STOPS SHORT! 25

BROAD-MINDED OR CONSCIENCE-
 STRETCHING 26

I DON'T HAVE TO HATE ANYMORE 27

GIVE TO SUCCEED 28

REMEMBER WHERE YOU CAME FROM 29

BUSINESS AND FLOWERS 30

I REMEMBER THE LAUGHTER 31

TRUTH FOR A HAPPY LIFE 32

ON THE ROAD AGAIN 33

HELP FOR THE IMPOSSIBLE 34

THE DIFFERENCE BETWEEN LIVING
 AND DYING 35

100+ ONE-MINUTE THOUGHT MANAGERS

TRUMPETS IN THE MORNING	36
CUT-FLOWER GENERATION	37
SOMETHING WORTH HOLDING ON TO HOLDS YOU	38
WHAT'S WORTH LETTING OUT?	39
TAKE ANOTHER LOOK	40
IF YOU THINK YOU ARE	41
A SPECIAL PLACE IN HELL	42
REJECTION	43
WATCH FOR THE BURNING BUSHES TODAY	44
PASS THE SALT FIRST	45
ALBERTA HUNTER'S SERMON	46
VULNERABILITY	47
AGONY, THEN GLORY	48
SAY "HELLO" TO GOD	49
HAD ANY FUN TODAY?	50
THANKFULNESS IMPROVES VISION	51
DON'T MISS LIVING	52
I'VE HAD ENOUGH OF THE NEGATIVE	53
A TRUE MEASURE	54
QUIT FLYING AGAINST REALITY	55
GIVE WHAT SHE REALLY WANTS	56
THE SPECIAL PLEASURES OF WOMANHOOD	57
A PERFECT MARRIAGE ATTITUDE	58
FAILING TOWARD SUCCESS	59

WHAT YOU ARE THINKING, YOU
    ARE BECOMING 60

THE WHAT AND WHEN OF GRACE 61

WHEN YOU ARE LOOKING FOR GOD 62

WHEN THE DEVIL SWEATS 63

SHAPED FOR HIGHER THINGS 64

LIFE'S STRANGEST GIFT 65

WHAT MATTERS TO PEOPLE 66

THE MAN WITH THE SMILING BIBLE 67

A REALLY GOOD GIFT 68

SHOCKINGLY POSITIVE... 69

TROUBLE IS NO SURPRISE 70

A SAFE PLACE FOR EVERYTHING............................. 71

IT WILL BE WORTH IT ALL 72

AVOIDING THE SWEATS OF LIFE.............................. 73

A TWO-CENT LAUGH 74

WELCOME FOR A HIPPIE 75

A SILVER TRUMPET DREAM 76

WHAT TO DO UNTIL THE WORLD ENDS 77

GOT A LIGHT?.. 78

SEEING WHAT IS OUT OF SIGHT 79

SINGLE SHORT CANDLE.. 80

COMMUNICATE.. 81

THE SUPREME COURT JUSTICE AND
    DUCK HUNTING.. 82

100+ ONE-MINUTE THOUGHT MANAGERS

GIVE SOMEBODY A GOLDEN APPLE TODAY 83

DADDY'S BOOK 84

RETROSPECT 85

GETTING BACK YOUR DEAD 86

HELPING A KID WITH HIS TRICYCLE 87

HAVING IT OUR WAY 88

BE AN ANGEL 89

WHERE IS HAPPINESS? 90

LIFE WORTH LIVING? 91

ENCOURAGEMENT FOR LIVING 92

WHERE ARE YOU SAFE? 93

WHEN WE FLY AGAIN 94

WAIT TIL YOU GET CLOSE ENOUGH
   TO JUDGE 95

FLOP PROOF 96

PRAYER HELPS YOU TALK BETTER 97

NO LOSE FIGHTS AT HOME 98

COMING BACK GOD'S WAY 99

NO SEPARATION, NO WAY 100

WHERE IS GRANDDADDY? 101

WHAT'S WORSE THAN HAVING NO VOICE? 102

ON GOD AND STONES 103

SUNDAY'S COMING! 104

PRAYER ABOUT "THINGS" OR ME 105

WHO'S TO SAY WHO'S TO BLAME 106

OF BEGGARS AND BREAD 107

WHEN SCRATCHING FOR IT WON'T HELP 108

EATING BY GRACE... 109

JUMP WITH ALL YOUR HEART 110

STRANGE THING ABOUT JESUS................................. 111

LOOK UP … AND REST 112

THE ATMOSPHERE OF A GOOD MEAL 113

THE DANGER OF INCONSIDERATION..................... 114

REMEMBER WHO IS BACKING YOU 115

PURPOSE HAS LIFE-GIVING POWER 116

DON'T EAT WITH THE CHICKENS 117

YOU CAN MAKE IT TODAY 118

ONE MORE ROUND! 119

HOW TO SETTLE YOUR STOMACH.......................... 120

GRACIOUS GLANDS 121

WHEN FORGIVENESS IS REAL................................... 122

ANOTHER VOICE TO HEAR FROM 123

LEARN TO SHIFT TO A PLAY MODE 124

GIVE GOD HIGH VISIBILITY 125

BLOOD ON THE FILE 126

BREAKING A FALSEHOOD CYCLE 127

LIFE-SAVING LAUGH 128

A WAY INTO THE PRESENCE OF KINGS 129

TAKE A MINUTE FOR YOURSELF.............................. 130

HOW TO HANDLE TEARS.. 131

RELATIONSHIPS AND DISAGREEMENTS 132

STRIKE A BLOW AGAINST EVIL 133

NEUTRALITY AND HELL 134

— A NOTE FROM THE AUTHOR —

The following anecdotes have been accumulated over the years. Therefore, the format from one to the other may differ and is just a reflection of the passage of time. Any examples not written down at the time are based on my best memory. Most quoted scripture comes from the King James Version of the Good Book. If I have paraphrased any scripture, I almost always use quotes and give the reader reference to the book, chapter, and verse of inspiration. In a few instances, I have capitalized the pronouns "he" and "him" when it is referencing our Lord and God. I have cited other works and authors where appropriate but also rely on public domain, free use, and the reader's understanding of inclusions that are not obviously my own.

DR. VANDER WARNER, JR.

— FOREWORD —

We tend to think that the significant decisions that shape our lives are settled only by extended retreats and ponderous thinking, perhaps aided by meditation on the things the great thinkers have written. True, there is some of that, but let's face it: it is more likely that a one-line statement triggered the mechanism of your decision. The nickel dropped, and forever afterward, you saw something you hadn't thought about before, felt differently about, and proceeded quite differently. I have several such lifechanging comments that have come to me. Sometimes, these thoughts come from an esteemed friend or counselor; at other times, they come from deep down inside me as various components of thought merge and distill into one clear, bottom-line principle.

Let's take it a step further. If you have not experienced such a life-changing minute, surely you have seen a disagreement resolved and friendship restored by one sentence that seemed to take both sides of the issue in sensitive hands and knit them into a seamless robe of reconciliation to throw around the concerns of both parties and warm them for days to come.

It is almost invariably true that things are not what you think they are, but what you think...they are, and what we tell ourselves about them is what becomes real to us. I have set forth, in this book, some things that help me think things into being what they ought to be. Of course, it is entirely possible that things were that way all the time, and I just brought my thinking to groove with reality. In either case, managing my thoughts was crucial.

I read a line or two in a biography of Smith Wigglesworth,

who was a legend in his time for always being on "cloud nine." When he was asked the secret of his good temperament, he responded, "I never ask Smith Wigglesworth how he feels. I always tell him!" I disagree with some of Smith Wigglesworth's theology, but I sure do agree with his "feel-ology!"

I am learning (slowly) to tell myself some things about life rather than allowing myself to tell me. If you talk to yourself, and you do, you might as well tell yourself the best things you know.

It was my good friend, John Haggai, author of the bestseller *How To Win Over Worry*, who said, "Start talking and acting the way you want to be thinking and feeling, and soon you'll be thinking and feeling the way you are talking and acting."

I've never received a better word on thought management. I still drop that thought in my mental data bank every now and then, and it still works.

In short, I am learning to manage my thoughts. With apologies to the life-changing book for executives, *The One Minute Manager*, I have put together *The 100+ One-Minute Thought Managers*.

Dr. Jerri Sutton, an educational consultant for the United Nations, said she read these thoughts twelve times. At the end of her comments, she wrote, "Take a minute, read for a moment, change your perspective." I believe that … it happens all the time.

One minute a day is all it will take to read these brief renderings, but one of them may change, for the better, your thoughts and your life for the rest of the 1439 minutes of this day … and one day at a time is enough for anybody.

— PREFACE —

When I think of life-changing thoughts, I remember the one sentence Dr. Carl Bates shared with me when I was a young preacher ... "Don't ever quit when you feel like it." I have worked with people who frequently brought me to the "wanting to quit" stage. Had it not been for that advice, I would have missed many maturing experiences and some wonderful victories in life.

I began collecting one-sentence, thoughtful, sometimes profound, insights from many sources years ago. When I saw Dr. Andy Telford's Bible with all the fly leaves filled with interesting short pieces, I knew I had found a place to keep all the things that inspired or challenged me, so I began to fill the blank pages of my Bible.

Later, when for six months I did a one-minute inspirational spot in the middle of Paul Harvey's radio show, I had the basics for my material at hand.

The discipline of compressing a "worthwhile" thought in our daily life, which would be broadcast-worthy, was quite a challenge. The response to that daily broadcast helped me believe that I had succeeded.

If one, just one of these thoughts influences or changes your life for the better, it will be worth all it took to bring this book to your hands.

I have gone over each of these short pieces several times. In most cases where I had not included a verse of Scripture within the original piece, I have added one for those of you who share with me the conviction that there is nothing with more potential for changing our lives than a word from the Good Book.

I must also say before you begin that these are not all my

thoughts ... unless you consider them mine because I believe them and try to practice them. I have made an effort to give credit where I knew it was due. When I have failed, please forgive me and enjoy them anyway.

DR. VANDER WARNER, JR.

GIVE ME THAT
OLD-TIME RELIGION

Everybody knows the old Gospel song, "Give Me That Old-Time Religion."

It has a lot of verses like, "It was good for my mother and father ... and it's good enough for me." That song has a lot more depth than you get at first glance. You see, the only religion worth having is one that has stood the test of time and eternity, one that can take you through the struggles of life.

Here is the greatest comment on faith or religion I've ever heard ... I mean the greatest.

"Only that faith is worth holding which has validity in the face of imminent death."

Let's run that through again ...

"Only that faith is worth holding which has validity in the face of imminent death."

"Gimme that ole time religion ... it will do when I am dying ... it will do when I am dying. It's good enough for me!"

WHAT'S DRIVING YOU

The other day, I was driving toward my office in my three year old, half-paid-for, disappointing clunker of a car.

A sparkling silver BMW streaked by me. Covet ... covet ... covet! Well, maybe it was just admiration ...

"Why can't I afford one of those things? I've always wanted one."

The next car that passed me was a real clunker driven by an old codger. That thing was battered, dull, dusty, and old enough to vote ... but the bewhiskered old brother had a bright smile on his face.

Man, did I feel like an ungrateful something!

His face reflected a look of satisfaction at least equal to the driver of the BMW and far better than mine.

I learned something from his grizzly, satisfied look.

It's not what you are driving. It's what's driving you.

Not that I speak in respect
of want: for I have learned
in whatsoever state
I am, be content.
— Philippians 4:11

DR. VANDER WARNER, JR.

FAITH AT DAD'S FUNERAL

When my dad died, we had his funeral at First Baptist Church in Charlotte, North Carolina. As the family stepped inside the sanctuary, the great organ swelled out the strains of a favorite hymn:

"How firm a foundation, ye saints of the Lord; Is laid for your faith in His excellent Word. What more can He say than to you He hath said, To you who for refuge to Jesus have fled?"

Those words sounded different in the presence of my father's casket. I was reminded of all the good things the Lord hath said ..."The dead shall be raised again at the last day ..." and many others.

The point is, our faith is designed to hold us in the best and the worst of life if we will hold on to it.

A faith worth holding will hold you.

DON'T AGREE WITH CAN'T-ERS

When discouragement begins to set in, remember some of the great names in history and the obstacles they faced and overcame.

As one working at writing, I've found encouragement from learning that Louisa May Alcott, author of *Little Women*, was told by an editor that she had no talent for writing and advised her to stick to her sewing. When Walt Disney submitted his first drawings for publication, the editor told him he had no artistic ability. Thomas Edison's teachers sent him home with a note telling his parents that their son was too stupid to learn. F. W. Woolworth, at twenty-one years of age, was not allowed to wait on the customers in the store where he worked. His employer told him that he didn't have enough sense to meet the public, but yet he built a great chain of stores.

Point! You can, even though they say you can't, as long as you don't agree with them!

Jesus said unto him, If thou canst believe, all things are possible to him that believeth.
—*Mark 9:23*

THE DEVIL'S BEST TOOL

Here's a great story about the devil. He advertised that his tools were for sale. On the date of the sale, the tools were displayed for public inspection, each being marked with its sale price. There was hatred, envy, jealousy, deceit, lying, pride, etc. Over to one side was a harmless-looking tool, well-worn but priced much higher than the others.

"What's the name of this tool?" a purchaser asked.

"That is discouragement," replied the devil.

"Why have you priced it so high?"

"Because it is more useful to me than the others. I can pry open and get inside a man's heart with that when I cannot get near him with the other tools. Once I get inside, I can make him do what I choose. It is badly worn because I use it on almost everyone since few people know it belongs to me."

The devil's price for the "tool of discouragement" was so high that it was never sold. He still has it, but he'll be happy to let you borrow it.

Why art thou cast down, O my soul? and why art thou disquieted within me? hope thou in God: for I shall yet praise him, who is the health of my countenance, and my God.
—Psalm 42:11

WHEN YOU THINK YOU ARE THROUGH

Years ago, I came into a classroom for a final exam on a course in Communism. While waiting for the professor, I went through as many of my notes as possible. On the exam was a question I could not have answered without that last-minute cram session. It made a whole letter grade difference. That reminds me of one of my personal life-changing thoughts …"It's what you do after you think you are through that makes the difference."

So, after you have done all you can, is there one more thing you can do? What about one more thing to get that relationship right … one more thing to succeed in your job … one more thing before you split … one more thing before you quit?

Jesus said, "Go one mile more than is required." Do you feel like you are through? Okay, do one more thing!

And whosoever shall compel thee
to go a mile, go with him twain.
—Matthew 5:41

DR. VANDER WARNER, JR.

FIND THE KITCHEN

Did you hear about the husband who was going to help with things around the house since his wife was in bed with the flu? He said, "Now, don't worry about a thing. I'm going to fix the kids something to eat, then I'll fix our supper. I'll take care of everything. Now, to begin with, where did you say the kitchen was?"

Funny, funny, but close to the truth. Some of us men don't know a whole lot about the kitchen, but if we value the extraordinary job our wives do there, we had better show it.

The Bible says, "Husbands, likewise, dwell with them with understanding ..." (1 Peter 3:7, NKJV).

One way to *under-stand* her is to *stand-under* her.

And ... Oh, the kitchen?

It's right over there.

LIFE'S MOST INFLUENTIAL VOICE

Every one of us has a very important person to talk to every day—ourselves.

It's probably true that the most influential voice we'll hear today is our own inner voice. So what are you telling yourself?

The Bible tells about a successful farmer who had a bumper crop. He thought to himself, "What shall I do? I have nowhere to store all my goods." So he decided to build a bigger barn—KEEP IT ALL FOR SELF.

Then he said, "I have much good laid up for many years. Take thine ease."

The death angel came and said, "Thou fool, this night thy soul is required of thee: then whose shall those things be which thou has provided?" (Luke 12:20).

The Scriptural bottom line is, "So is he that layeth up treasure for himself, and is not rich toward God" (Luke 20:21).

The point: When you talk to yourself, tell yourself the truth and have an intelligent conversation with yourself. When you talk to yourself, YOU are really listening!

DR. VANDER WARNER, JR.

KEEP YOUR PIT STOPS SHORT!

In the big auto races, the Indy 500 and others, time for pit stops is crucial. Those crews have practiced the repair or re-fuel stops until it's a matter of seconds, rarely minutes.

You can win or lose the race by the length of your pit stops.

There is a lesson for all of life in that. You can't win or succeed in life if you allow yourself to stay in the pits all the time!

The Bible says in Psalm 40:1–3, "he inclined unto me, and heard my cry. He brought me up out of a horrible pit ... and put a new song in my mouth."

So, one of life's great lessons is "don't succumb to pit-dom."

Keep your pit stop short. Refuel, repair, and be on your way.

Stay in the race!

BROAD-MINDED OR CONSCIENCE-STRETCHING

I was talking with a friend about the awful language in an otherwise fabulous movie—great story, creative production, and an inspiring ending.

When I said that I was bothered by the scatological language, the young person with whom I talked said, "I didn't pay any attention to it. I didn't even notice."

Well, I'm no prude. I lived in a fraternity house at Wake Forest University, but that stuff bothered me.

We are living in a day when we are sometimes taught in college that there is no right and wrong. The Bible says that wrong communication can corrupt good manners (1 Corinthians 15:33). I ran across an old line I'd written down from somewhere that helps me in this area: "Some people think their mind is broadening when actually their conscience is stretching."

---

*Be not deceived: evil
communications corrupt
good manners.*
—1 Corinthians 15:33

DR. VANDER WARNER, JR.

I DON'T HAVE TO HATE ANYMORE

Some time ago, a tall, tough-looking, black leather jacketed boy began to attend service in my church. He was a member of the Hell's Angels motorcycle club.

The truth from the Bible began to clear up his preconceived notions about God, life, and people. His search for identity and reality ended in Jesus, who is the truth. He changed his membership from Hell's Angels to my church.

Later, he gave a testimonial of his journey.

He concluded with a great smile on his heretofore scowling face as he said, "It's wonderful to know that I don't have to hate anymore!"

When you've experienced love, you can love!

If ye keep my commandments,
ye shall abide in my love; even as
I have kept my Father's commandments,
and abide in his love.
—John 15:10

GIVE TO SUCCEED

In a review of a book about Howard Hughes, the review concluded with this sentence: "This book documents the abysmal failure of a man who could buy anything but had nothing to sell." Tragic!

If we spend our lives in "getting to keep" and no time working for something to give ... the time will come when we have nothing for which to live.

Jesus said, *"Give, and it shall be given unto you" (Luke 6:38).*

I've discovered in life that the things that make it all worthwhile are the things that someone has to give me, if I have them at all ... love, appreciation, acceptance, honor, friendship, etc.

You can't buy that stuff, but life is not worth living without it, and we don't get it 'til we give it.

Give, and it shall be given unto you;
good measure, pressed down, and
shaken together, and running over, shall
men give into your bosom. For with the same
measure that ye mete withal it shall
be measured to you again.
—Luke 6:38

DR. VANDER WARNER, JR.

REMEMBER WHERE YOU CAME FROM

Loretta Lynn, the country music superstar, lived on a sprawling farm in the south. Her house is a gigantic, white mansion where she has maids and groundskeepers. On one corner of the farm stands an old, dilapidated shack, which is the abandoned dwelling place of some unfortunate soul of the past. Loretta had insisted that the shack be preserved intact. She often strolled to it, entered it, and contemplated her childhood. The shack reminded her of where she was brought up and of the miserable living conditions that instilled in her the still-present quest for survival. The old shack served to make her truly thankful for what she had.

Most of us have some kind of old shack in our memory. The one I have in my memory makes me thankful for what I have today.

Paul the Apostle said, "This is a faithful saying, and worthy of all acceptation, that Christ Jesus came into the world to save sinners; of whom I am chief" (1 Timothy 1:15).

BUSINESS AND FLOWERS

B. J. Thomas is my wife's favorite country singer. I haven't decided whether it's his looks or his singing, but he sings a song with a line that intrigues me. "You better take care of business, Mr. Businessman." That's in the Bible: "If you see a man diligent in business, he shall stand before the mighty" (Proverbs 22:29, paraphrased).

He goes on to describe a workaholic who is after his secretary, has a harlot on the side, has no time for his children, and is playing accounting tricks with his bookkeeper.

B. J. Thomas asks a couple of gripping questions like "Did you notice your children growing?" but one of the most gripping questions in the song asks, "… did you catch the scent of those roses in your garden?"

I have a demanding and engrossing job, but I'm going to take time to enjoy the flowers.

So help me, God!

And that's the kind of help it takes!

Be still, and know
that I am God:
—Psalm 46:10a

DR. VANDER WARNER, JR.

I REMEMBER THE LAUGHTER

Have you helped anyone have a good laugh lately? Do you remember the last time you enjoyed laughter?

I invited a great teacher and internationally known author to my church some time ago. When he said he could put me on his schedule, I said, "Great! I can't wait 'til you get here. I want to laugh with you some."

Well, Vance Havner came and did a great job for us at church. There were many inspiring moments and profound concepts dealt with, and many lives were changed.

But, most of all, *I remember the laughter!*

The Good Book says, "A merry heart doeth good like a medicine" (Proverbs 17:22a). That's a medicine that doesn't need a spoonful of sugar to make it go down.

Joe E. Brown said, "If you have to be dirty to be funny, then you're not funny, just dirty."

Give someone a great body-shaking laugh today and have a good laugh yourself.

It's biblical.

TRUTH FOR A HAPPY LIFE

I have an old-fashioned mother who loves, carries, reads, and lives by the Bible. She does not have a great deal of formal education, but she does have wisdom, a happy life, and happy children.

Here's a little poem I think about when I think of her:

We search the world for truth,
We call the good, the bad,
From graven stone and written scroll,
And all old-fashioned fields of the soul.
And weary seekers of the best,
We come back laden from our quest,
To find that all the sages said,
Are in the Book our mothers read.

Before you give up in your search for a "happy life," examine the truths of the Bible. It's been around a long time.

Then said Jesus to those Jews which believed on him, If ye continue in my word, then are ye my disciples indeed; And ye shall know the truth, and the truth shall make you free.
—John 8:31–32

DR. VANDER WARNER, JR.

ON THE ROAD AGAIN

Remember that country song, "On the Road Again"?
Willie Nelson made enough on that one to get a haircut and shave.

We all get off the road now and then, but it's only terrible and devastating if we don't get back on. Sometimes, being off shows us how we can really enjoy being on the right road.

To know you are on the right road is a fine thing, but to return *to it* after being on the wrong road multiplies the pleasure. Come on back. You'll be welcome!

Remember the Prodigal Son!

For this my son was dead, and
is alive again; he was lost, and
is found. And they began to be merry.
—Luke 15:24

HELP FOR THE IMPOSSIBLE

A man was in the hospital visiting his buddy who was wound in bandages from head to toe ... arm in a sling ... leg in traction!

His buddy asked him, "What happened to me?"

"Well, we were both drunk, and you opened the window on the eighth floor and said, 'I'm going to jump out of this window and fly around this building,' and you jumped."

"Why didn't you stop me?" asked the patient.

His friend replied, "I thought you could do it."

No amount of positive thinking by brains dulled by drugs, ignorance, or false premises can change the fact that if we are going to fly, we must have help.

The next best thing to being able to do the impossible is being friends with the One who can.

Nothing is impossible with God!

And Jesus looking upon them saith,
With men it is impossible, but not
with God: for with God
all things are possible.
—Mark 10:27

DR. VANDER WARNER, JR.

THE DIFFERENCE BETWEEN LIVING AND DYING

Here is the most unusual funeral I ever heard about. The man being buried had done well in life. He had made some money and bought the dream of his lifetime—a gold Cadillac.

His last request was to be buried in that car.

So, at the enormously large grave, a great crane was rented for the job. They dressed him in his best suit, propped him up behind the wheel, and lowered the dead man in the gold Cadillac slowly into the ground.

Two of his old cronies, who had not done so well, stood watching the scene. As the gleaming car dropped into the ground, one said to the other, "Man, ain't that living!"

No, that's dying!

Now, there's a problem: some folks don't know the difference between living and dying.

Jesus saith unto him,
I am the way, the truth and the life:
no man cometh unto
the Father, but by me.
—John 14:6

TRUMPETS IN THE MORNING

There is a fabulous Jewish legend about hell that goes like this:

When Michael the Archangel asked Satan, who was cast out of heaven, what he missed most now that he was in hell, Satan replied, "Most of all, I miss the trumpets in the morning."

Life without joy and zing is so awful that every day, somebody opts to end it all and escape through suicide. Who doesn't want to get out of hell? But what a hell it leaves behind for "the people you don't want to hurt!"

We were designed to have joy in life, "… hear the trumpets." That's why Jesus said, "These things have I spoken unto you, that my joy might remain in you, and that your joy might be full" (John 15:11).

DR. VANDER WARNER, JR.

CUT-FLOWER GENERATION

I think it was the brilliant Quaker philosopher Elton Trueblood who described society in the '60s as the "cut flower generation."

In those days, there was a rejection of the old—old things, old ways, and old values. It almost killed us as a nation.

I had an orange tree once that I raised from seeds. It sprouted in a tin can, and I transplanted it into larger containers, one after another. The tree would go into shock for a while, then flourish and grow, and I would transplant it again.

One summer, I made two transplantings—that orange tree died. Cause of death: too much moving!

David said that a man who sinks his roots in the truth is like a tree whose leaf does not wither (Psalm 1:3). It doesn't sound right, but it's true—you can't move till your roots are ready!

SOMETHING WORTH
HOLDING ON TO ... HOLDS YOU

A line I read in Esquire years ago stated, "A man becomes conservative precisely at that point where he has something to preserve."

There's a line in Scripture that reads, "Test all things; hold fast what is good" (1 Thessalonians 5:21, NKJV).

It does take a bit of growing and a bit of maturing before we realize we have something worth holding on to:

A line beyond which we will not go ...

A belief we will not yield on ...

A value we will not change ...

A conviction that is settled for us ...

A principle we will not compromise ...

Something worth holding on to.

Until we have some of these things worth holding, we really don't have much to hold on to.

And nothing to hold us.

DR. VANDER WARNER, JR.

WHAT'S WORTH LETTING OUT?

I was preparing to go to England for some teaching there, and my research included a conversation with a nineteen-year-old English lad—the son of a doctor who was visiting the United States.

I had read that only between two percent and three percent of Britons ever attend church. On the basis of that, I asked the young Englishman, "Why have the British lost their faith?"

His face became flushed, and glistening tears rimmed his eyes slightly as he said very quietly, "Sir, they haven't lost their faith … it's just way down deep inside."

You know what I really believe? I believe that's true for nearly everybody—yes, some you would never imagine.

What about this? If faith is worth keeping deep inside, it's worth letting out. Somebody you care about might be happily surprised and encouraged.

Let the redeemed of the Lord say so,
whom he hath redeemed from
the hand of the enemy;
—Psalm 107:2

TAKE ANOTHER LOOK

Remember when Walter Cronkite used to sign off the evening news with: "… and that's the way it is, this tenth day of September, nineteen, whatever"?

An old country preacher, way out in the "boonies," watching his snowy old set, as Walter said, "And that's the way it is" one night, hollered back, "No, that's the way it looks."

There's a shocking verse from Proverbs that reads, "There is a way that seems right to man, But its end is the way of death" (Proverbs 14:12, NKJV).

Take another look at what you are getting ready to give your life and time to.

It might just look like it's worth it. The way it looks may not be the "way it is."

DR. VANDER WARNER, JR.

IF YOU THINK YOU ARE

One of life's most important questions is: "What do you think?"

If you think you are beaten, you are;
If you think you dare not, you don't;
If you'd like to win but think you can't;
It's almost a cinch you won't.
Life's battles don't always go
To a stronger or faster man;
But sooner or later the man who wins,
Is the one who thinks he can.

Long ago, that truth came from God's heart this way: "For as he thinketh in his heart, so is he" (Proverbs 23:7a).

You may not be what you think you are, but what you think you are.

A SPECIAL PLACE IN HELL

Here is one of my all-time big thoughts—I mean a real "biggie"!

"There is a special place reserved in hell for those who, in a moment of moral crisis, remain neutral."

A little poem applies this:

No enemy! The boast is poor!
You've hit no traitor on the hip,
You've dashed no cup from perjured lip,
You've never turned a wrong to right,
You've been a traitor in the fight!

The Book above all books says, "Having done all ... stand" (Ephesians 6:13b, NKJV).

Now, today, my friend, don't be afraid to stand *for what's right!*

REJECTION

Rejection—the emotional pain of rejection is about as tough as anything we humans experience. If you don't believe it, ask someone whose spouse left them in shock and walked out for someone else.

I remember so vividly when I was a second-grader and in love with that fascinating and confident blond seven-year-old.

I was looking at her when she looked my way and spoke. I thought, *To me?* So I said, "Me?"

She scowled and said, "I'll never mean you," and looked beyond me to another kid. I don't even remember who it was, but that moment of rejection was etched permanently in my mind.

I can't avoid rejection from others from time to time, but I can pray, "Good Lord, don't let me reject one of your creatures that way."

Love one another as
I have loved you.
—John 15:12b

WATCH FOR THE
BURNING BUSHES TODAY

The story of Moses and the burning bush is the story of God caring so much that He would do whatever it took to get the attention of a man He was going to use to rescue a whole nation.

When Moses saw the bush burning without being consumed, he couldn't understand it, so he stayed to see what it was, and the God of Abraham, Isaac, and Jacob redirected his whole life.

Watch for burning bushes in your life. The things you can't explain, the things that grab your attention, the things that hurt, shock, wound, or that make no sense at all and may seem so useless. Stop and turn, take a thoughtful look—and wait—and listen.

See if God is trying to get through to you. If He is, you don't want to miss it.

I will stand upon my watch,
and set me upon the tower,
and will watch to see what he
will say unto me, and what
I shall answer when
I am reproved.
—Habakkuk 2:1

DR. VANDER WARNER, JR.

PASS THE SALT FIRST

In a great piece of literature on love is this statement: "Love is kind." The point is, if you want to express love to someone, being kind is one way.

Someone defined kindness as "courtesy in little things." Some of you can relate to the wife of a busy public figure. When she was asked if her husband remembered the big events of the family, she replied, "Yes, he never forgets an anniversary or birthday, but he forgets to pass me the salt. I have a birthday only once a year, but I need the salt three times a day!"

Hey, fellow American male, pass her the salt first today! It says, "I love you!"

Say it once again—with salt!

And be ye kind one to another, tenderhearted, even as God for Christ's sake hath forgiven you.
—Ephesians 4:32

ALBERTA HUNTER'S SERMON

Alberta Hunter was some woman. A great, unsurpassed blues singer. She had a comeback at the age of eighty.

My friend, Hatcher Story, took me to New York to the Eatery, a restaurant in Greenwich Village, to hear her sing. Her sense of rhythm, timing, and humor was flawless. Her love for the crowd was unmistakable, and when she talked, you wanted to listen.

She delivered little hard-hitting sermonettes between the musical sets. In that Greenwich Village night spot, I was jealous. I heard "Amens."

Few preachers ever hear such sounds.

She said, "Children, if you've been away from home a long time, write home to your mommy and daddy. Write home, children. Somebody back there loves you and wants to hear how you are."

Is that biblical? Oh, yes, to communicate love is clearly in the Bible.

DR. VANDER WARNER, JR.

VULNERABILITY

I have a friend who said he was never accepted in his church as pastor until, at a church party, someone hit him in the face with a pie. What happened was they saw he was not untouchable ... he became vulnerable ... open.

I've heard a fair number of wives say, "He doesn't need me ... he never talks to me," and one said, "We never chit-chat."

One beautiful young woman explained to me why she had an affair with a not-so-hot-looking guy when she had a double for Robert Redford for a husband. She said, "But the other guy talks to me. He makes me feel important. He shares."

When the stresses are terrific, and you really need someone ... they will be there ... if you've been there.

AGONY, THEN GLORY

I collect prayers. Jim Elliot, a college student who went on to die by the hands of the people he went to help, wrote this prayer in a birthday greeting to his brother:

"For you, brother, I pray that the Lord might crown this year with His goodness, and in the coming one give you a hallowed, dare-devil spirit in lifting the biting sword of truth ... consuming you with a passion that is called by the cultured citizens of Christendom 'Fanaticism,' but known to God as saintly madness that led His Son through bloody sweat and hot tears to agony on a crude cross ... and Glory."

Most glory ... worth having ... follows agony by somebody. An old warrior wrote, "If we suffer with Him ... we reign with Him."

SAY "HELLO" TO GOD

I had a lovely visit to a home where there were two little boys. As we were saying our goodbyes, one of the little boys called out to me in his crystal-clear voice, "Say hello to God!"

I've thought and thought about that statement. He saw me as a person on speaking terms with Almighty God. It's true for me, and it's true for you—speaking terms with God!

Yes, you see, it's not all that much based on who you are or what kind of person you are, but on what He is like.

King David said, "This poor man cried, and the Lord heard him and saved him out of all his troubles."

Try it. You'll see. God will hear you.

Say "hello" to God today ... and every day!

Hear my cry, O God;
attend unto my prayer.
—Psalm 61:1

HAD ANY FUN TODAY?

Here's a word to encourage you to live the good life now... don't wait. Have a day filled with "fun."

We squander health in search of wealth,
We work and skimp and save.
Then squander wealth in search of health,
And all we get a grave.

When I finished writing that, from way down deep in my memory, I could hear the childish voice from long ago of one of my now-grown daughters saying, "Didn't we have fun today, Daddy!"

I don't remember when that was said or by which daughter. It's been a long time.

I only wish I had more times in my bank of memories when someone I love said, "Didn't we have fun today!"

Let every one of us please
his neighbour for his good
to edification.
—Romans 15:2

THANKFULNESS IMPROVES VISION

Some years ago, I was standing on a little balcony outside my hotel room, looking at the skyline of Cairo, just across the Nile.

The early morning haze obscured things in the distance, but I took a picture of that ancient city of the Pharaohs.

When I later flashed that slide on the screen, I saw something I had not seen that morning. In the distance were the pyramids. My amber lens filter had cut through the haze to that fabulous scene.

What a surprise!

On this day, things you've never seen before, good things, may appear if you look through the filter of thankfulness.

There's a verse in the Bible that says, "be thankful in everything." Oh, it may not change things, but it will change how you see them.

Giving thanks always for all
things unto God and the Father
in the name of our
Lord Jesus Christ.
—Ephesians 5:20

DON'T MISS LIVING

There's a wonderful book on the market entitled *David.* It is a heart-breaking ... heart-mending story of the great courage of little David Rothenberg.

On March 3, 1983, a frustrated young father poured kerosene over the body of his little six-year-old son in his bed and struck a match to it.

When it was over, the little boy had third-degree burns over ninety percent of his body. He was massively and hideously burned, but he lived!

That courageous little lad gave us one of the greatest sentences of all time. He said, "I didn't miss living. That's wonderful enough for me."

I didn't miss living!

The Master Teacher said, "I've come that you might have life" (John 10:10).

Nothing "coming down" is worth it if it keeps us from really living!

DR. VANDER WARNER, JR.

I'VE HAD ENOUGH OF
THE NEGATIVE

Two prisoners stood looking out their cell window after a rain. One of them remarked about the mud and puddles and dreary dampness just outside their cell.

His cellmate, looking a little farther out from the cell window, said, "But look how the flowers have brightened, and the grass is so much greener."

Somebody's mother always said, "It's all in the way you look at it."

Do you see the flowers or the mud?

Paul the Apostle said, "… whatsoever things are pure … whatsoever things are lovely, whatsoever things are of good report … think on these things" (Philippians 4:8).

I hear you, Paul! If I never focus on the negative again, it'll be fine. I've done it enough for a lifetime.

A TRUE MEASURE

In 1935, a Nazi district leader said, "In later centuries, when one will have a true measure for things as they are today, it will be said, 'Christ was great, but Adolph Hitler was greater.'"

Hitler himself said, "One is either a German or a Christian. You cannot be both. Do you really believe the masses will ever be Christian again? Nonsense! Never again! That tale is finished. No one will ever listen to it again."

Hum?

The world has never missed a December singing Christmas carols, even after Hitler made that statement.

Talk about your true measure ...

That old, old story is still "Good News."

Jesus said, "Heaven and earth shall pass away, but my words shall not pass away" (Matthew 24:35).

QUIT FLYING AGAINST REALITY
TALK TO SOMEBODY ... THEN LISTEN

There is a beautiful little bird, a flycatcher, that keeps flying from the dogwood up against my window, time after time. He's done that for several days. Why is he doing that? Well, he doesn't see things as they really are. He thinks the reflection of the dogwood in the window is another tree, and he keeps trying to perch there.

One of the most important tasks in life is to get an accurate picture of what's going on. If you don't, you'll keep making wrong decisions. You'll keep flying against reality. You'll keep wondering what's going wrong.

The best thing I know to do is to find somebody who loves you, who has a track record of wisdom, and lay it out before them ... ask them what's going on. Then do that again with another person who loves you.

The Bible says there is safety in a multitude of counselors. Find somebody to talk to and then listen.

That little bird just flew against the window again—he has nobody to talk to.

Call unto me, and I will answer
thee, and show thee great and
mighty things, which thou
knowest not.
—Jeremiah 33:3

GIVE WHAT SHE REALLY WANTS

If we love each other in marriage, we want to be a part of what makes each other happy. We sometimes get off-track and deceived into believing that the happiness he or she wants comes from presents. After all, it thrilled her when you gave her that last gift.

Dr. James Dobson, the famous psychologist, in his research on that, comes up with a surprising conclusion.

He asks and answers, "What do women want from their husbands? It is not a bigger home, a better dishwasher, or a newer automobile; rather, it is the assurance that 'hand in hand,' we'll face the best and worst that life has to offer ... together."

The best marital guidebook in the world counsels us to love our wives like Jesus loved and gave Himself for us. That's the key ... give yourself.

Husbands, love your wives, even
as Christ also loved the church,
and gave himself for it.
—Ephesians 5:25

DR. VANDER WARNER, JR.

THE SPECIAL PLEASURES
OF WOMANHOOD

Joyce Landorf in *His Stubborn Love* wrote, "If I could write a prescription for the women of the world, I would provide each one with a healthy dose of self-esteem and person-worth. I have no doubt that this is their greatest need. If women felt genuinely respected in their role as wives and mothers, they would not need to abandon it for something better. If they felt equal with men in personal worth, they would not need to be equivalent to men in responsibility. If they could only bask in the dignity and status granted them by the Creator, then their femininity would be valued as their greatest asset rather than scorned as an old garment to be discarded."

Without question, the future of a nation depends on how it sees its women, and I hope we will teach our little girls to be glad they were chosen by God ...

For the special pleasures of womanhood!

Who can find a virtuous woman?
for her price is far above rubies.
—Proverbs 31:10

A PERFECT MARRIAGE ATTITUDE

James Dobson in *What Wives Wish Their Husbands Knew About Women* writes:

"Can you accept the fact that your husband will never be able to meet all of your needs and aspirations? Seldom does one human being satisfy every longing and hope in the breast of another. Obviously, this coin has two sides: You can't be his perfect woman either. He is no more equipped to resolve your entire package of emotional needs than you are to become his sexual dream machine every twenty-four hours. Both partners have to settle for human foibles, faults, irritabilities, fatigue, and occasional nighttime 'headaches.' A good marriage is not one where perfection reigns: it is a relationship where a healthy perspective overlooks a multitude of 'unresolvables.'"

A perfect marriage is not one without problems ... it's one with a perfect attitude toward problems.

Nevertheless let every one of you
in particular so love his wife
even as himself; and the wife
see that she reverence her husband.
—Ephesians 5:33

FAILING TOWARD SUCCESS

One of the most common causes of discouragement is failure. Although no one enjoys failing, the act of failure is not nearly as bad as we usually think it is. In fact, when failure is properly understood, it is not something to be avoided; rather, it should be understood as a positive aid, for success is not the absence of failure. Failure may be the stepping stone of success. We may fail our way to success.

You don't have to be a baseball fan to remember Babe Ruth, who, for a while, held the record for hitting home runs. He also holds another record: more strike-outs than any other player in the history of the sport. Thus, the Babe experienced the greatest failure rate in becoming one of baseball's all-time home run hitters!

Paul the Apostle said, "You can knock me down ... but you can't knock me out!" (2 Corinthians 4:9).

WHAT YOU ARE THINKING, YOU ARE BECOMING

On a trip to Hong Kong, Dr. Norman Vincent Peale came upon a tattoo parlor run by an elderly Chinese practitioner of this ancient art. He noticed in the window a display of the various tattoos that could be imprinted on your skin—flags, patriotic slogans, daggers, skulls, crossbones, etc., but an eye-catcher was "Born to lose." Curious, he asked the owner if people really requested that one. "Yes," he replied, "sometimes." The last customer who asked for it had it imprinted on his chest.

"Why on earth," Dr. Peale asked, "would anyone want to be branded with a gloomy slogan like that?"

The old Chinese proprietor shrugged and gave this penetrating answer: "Before tattoo on chest, tattoo on mind!"

The Bible is right about it. What you are thinking, you are becoming.

For as he thinketh in
his heart, so is he.
—Proverbs 23:7a

THE WHAT AND WHEN OF GRACE

Grace is a favorite word for religious people. It means "God's provision for your need." Someone once asked D. L. Moody if he had dying grace. "No," he replied, "now I have living grace, but when I come to die, I shall be given dying grace." He had learned that God gives us today what He knows we need to enable us to stand life's tests. As the poet says:

God broke the years to hours and days
That hour by hour and day by day,
Just going on a little way,
We might be able all along,
To keep quite strong.

There is a great old hymn whose second verse goes like this:

"Fear not, I am with thee: O be not dismayed, For I am thy God and will still give thee aid: I'll strengthen thee, help thee and cause thee to stand, Upheld by my righteous, omnipotent hand."

"Fear thou not; for I am with thee: be not dismayed; for I am thy God: I will strengthen thee; yea, I will help thee; yea, I will uphold thee with the right hand of my righteousness."

All of which is to say:

We can take life one grace at a time.

WHEN YOU ARE
LOOKING FOR GOD

If you've been searching for God lately, you've probably seen traces of Him in the stars, mountains, and in all growing things. There is too much order in the universe to have just happened by chance, but you don't find much personally satisfying there.

Where are you looking for God?

This poem may help:

> *I sought to hear the voice of God,*
> *And climbed the topmost steeple;*
> *But God declared,*
> *"Go down again,*
> *I dwell among the people."*

When trying to find God, you're likely to find Him among His first love: people. Then, if you want to do something for Him, remember that Jesus said, "Inasmuch as you have done it unto the least of these ... ye have done it unto me" (Matthew 25:40b).

DR. VANDER WARNER, JR.

WHEN THE DEVIL SWEATS

Allen T. Pierson told of watching a blacksmith working at his trade. With a small hammer, the smithy tapped the white-hot iron on the anvil and nodded to his helper to hit as hard as he could with a heavy sledgehammer.

The minister asked, "Why do you first dent it with such tiny taps?"

"Oh, I'm just showing him where to hit," was the reply.

Pierson thought for a moment and said, "I think we can draw a parable from your actions. Often, God puts a finger on the weak points in His servant's life or work and then permits the devil to bring down the sledgehammer blows of affliction to forge him into a stronger man and a better Christian; thus, He makes the devil sweat for the saint's benefit."

Is that what the Bible means when it says, "All things work together for our good?" (Romans 8:28).

SHAPED FOR HIGHER THINGS

However dark the "now" may be, there will be light enough in God's tomorrow to explain it all. The Good Book puts it: "… so we don't faint, we don't give up though our outward man perishes" (Isaiah 40:31).

A fellow minister wrote this:

"I have a friend who lost a job, a fortune, a wife, and a home during the depression, but tenaciously held to his faith … the only thing he had left. One day, he stopped to watch some men doing stonework on a huge church. Seeing a master craftsman chiseling a triangular piece of rock, he asked, 'What are you going to do with that?' The workman said, 'Do you see that little opening way up there near the spire? Well, I'm shaping this down here so that it will fit in up there!"

I think I'll accept that. God is getting me in shape today for higher things tomorrow.

LIFE'S STRANGEST GIFT

Here's a thought about life's strangest gift ... the gift of a thorn.

Paul said, "And lest I should be exalted above measure ... there was given to me a thorn in the flesh" (2 Corinthians 12:7).

What a strange gift Paul was given ... a sharp, irritating thorn, but it accomplished God's purpose by reminding the apostle that he was just a weak man. It hindered him, but it also humbled him. Whatever this affliction was, it contributed greatly to his character growth, for he wrote, "Most gladly therefore will I rather glory in my infirmities that the power of Christ may rest upon me" (2 Corinthians 12:9b).

If you are experiencing trials, accept them as coming from the Heavenly Father. Remember, "some of the most beautiful roses are found among the sharpest thorns."

Ouch! Here comes a rose.

WHAT MATTERS TO PEOPLE

I keep getting taught big lessons about what really matters to people.

When I sometimes return to former pastorates, I meet lovely young adults who were kids when I was there. I remember many of them, but not all that clearly.

I remember the buildings we built, the budgets we raised, the increase in attendance we had, and the celebrations we shared.

They don't. They never mention any of those things.

They mention the time I stopped and talked to them, the time I noticed them in church, the time I attended their meetings, the compliments or the quiet talks we had alone in my study.

Those were the times I made them feel like somebody that was important.

Funny how giving time and attention does that better than anything.

THE MAN WITH THE SMILING BIBLE

When "smiley faces" first came out as little stickers, I stuck one on the cover of my Bible. Using it in a preaching mission in England, the people wondered what it was. You couldn't tell from a distance. When I showed them, they immediately dubbed me "the man with the smiling Bible." They even wrote a song about me and my "smiling Bible."

The truth is that the Bible is designed to put a smile on your face. God loves you and provides a way for you to have a home in heaven and live a life without regrets in this life.

Yes, it's a Book that will make you smile, but you may have to cry first!

Weeping may endure for a night,
but joy cometh in the morning.
—Psalm 30:5b

Put a smile on your face.
Read the Bible!

A REALLY GOOD GIFT

Sometimes at weddings, just before the wedding prayer, with a hand on the head of the bride and groom, I say something like this to the wedding guests: "You have given this couple gifts individually. Now, let's everybody give them one together. Let's give them the gift of the best prayer that comes to our minds."

There is somebody you really love who needs that particular gift today. Don't worry about fancy wrappings like beautiful words. Prayer is like any other gift—it's the thought that counts. God is watching your heart, not your grammar. Give somebody the gift of the best prayer you can think of.

You'll also have the joy of knowing you've done what the Bible said ...

Pray for one another ...
—James 5:16a (NKJV)

SHOCKINGLY POSITIVE

When I was a lad, candy and snack salesmen still gave samples away—even to kids. You know, like the cigarette companies with their tiny packs.

On a sunny Saturday, my family and I, walking across a shopping mall parking lot, saw a Krispy Kreme doughnut truck. The man behind the wheel was filling out his forms. I had a thought from my childhood …

I walked up with a big smile and jokingly asked, "Got any samples?"

Not hesitating, with a bigger smile, he looked up and said with a cheery voice, "Got plenty of samples!" He reached down at the same time and handed me a box of doughnuts.

All I could say was, "Really?"

We had a good feeling for a long time about that.

Jesus went about shocking people all the time with positive responses to their deepest needs!

TROUBLE IS NO SURPRISE

I keep forgetting to expect some good along with the bad, and what happens is that I begin to think everything has gone wrong when just one thing goes wrong.

The Big Fisherman said, "Beloved, do not be surprised at the fiery trial among you, which is to try you, as though some strange thing were happening to you" (1 Peter 4:12).

In other words, it's the norm for even good people doing good things to experience some tough times. It's the nature of the universe. It's in all creation. So don't be shocked. The devil is trying to catch you off guard.

Quote him in this poem:

This old world is hard to beat
You get a thorn with every rose,
But ain't the roses sweet!

A SAFE PLACE FOR EVERYTHING

During the Depression, a once wealthy man who had lost it all was deeply discouraged when he heard their washer-woman scrubbing the clothes and singing, "Jesus never fails."

Shaking his head in disbelief, and with a little annoyance, he questioned her. "Becky, what are you singing about? You lost all your little savings too when the bank closed."

Looking up, wiping the sweat, she replied, "You're right, but God's bank ain't busted yet!"

Jesus said, "There's a place to invest where moths and rust don't corrupt nor thieves break through and steal" (Luke 12:33).

A good place to invest is in eternal security, where everything is safe forever!

IT WILL BE WORTH IT ALL

There is a line in the Bible that says, "If we die, we have a house not made with hands eternal in the heavens ..."

"Eternal in the heavens."

While the concept of eternity is difficult to take in, here is an attempt at describing it.

"High up in the north, in the land called Svithjod, there stands a rock. It is a hundred miles high and a hundred miles long. Once every 1,000 years, a little bird comes to this rock to sharpen its beak. When the rock has thus been worn away, then a single day of eternity will have gone by" (Hendrick von Loon, *The Story of Mankind,* 1921).

When the good Lord offers eternity in exchange for our life span, He offers a deal we can't afford to pass by.

---

*For we know that if our earthly
house of this tabernacle were
dissolved, we have a building of God,
an house not made with hands,
eternal in the heavens.
—2 Corinthians 5:1*

DR. VANDER WARNER, JR.

AVOIDING THE SWEATS OF LIFE

Over at West Broad Honda—home of my little Accord—is a pretty good man. He is the man who writes up the service orders. Over there one day, I waited while an irate customer complained, and the phones rang and rang while customers continued to line up. He was pulled here and there and in every and which direction.

When he got to me, I said, "Man, I don't see how you handle all this stuff." He looked surprised at what I'd said. It didn't look that way to him.

With a shrug of his shoulders, he said, "Oh, well, it isn't so bad." I mean, he was surprised that I thought it was bad.

Here is a living example of one of the greatest pieces of advice I ever received...are you ready for this?

Don't sweat the small stuff! Cause if you do, you're gonna go through life real sweaty.

Rejoice in the Lord always: and again
I say, Rejoice. Let your moderation be known
unto all men. The Lord is at hand. Be careful for nothing; but
in every thing by prayer and supplication with thanksgiving
let your requests be made known unto God. And the peace of
God, which passeth all understanding, shall keep your hearts
and minds through Christ Jesus. Finally, brethren, whatsoever things are true, whatsoever things are honest, whatsoever
things are just, whatsoever things are pure, whatsoever things
are lovely, whatsoever things are of good report; if there be
any virtue, and if there be any praise, think on these things.
—Philippians 4:4–8

A TWO-CENT LAUGH

One of the most memorable experiences of my life happened when I was a twelve-year-old country boy selling newspapers to the soldiers on maneuvers.

The paper I sold, *The Philadelphia Inquirer*, cost just three cents, and often, the soldier lads would give me the two cents change for a tip.

But my tender, boyish heart was crushed once when I didn't have the two cents in change, for the young soldier said, "Shoot, you're just saying that so you can keep the rest of the nickel." Tears came to my eyes nearly an hour later when I returned to that tent and gave him his two cents change.

I've thought about that a thousand times. I'm sure now that he was just kidding, but I didn't perceive it that way at the time.

I've learned something: kidding that crushes even a child is not worth the laugh.

Build a child today ... don't crush him.

And whosoever shall offend one of these
little ones that believe in me, it is
better for him that a millstone were hanged
about his neck, and he were cast into the sea.
—Mark 9:42

WELCOME FOR A HIPPIE

After being in jail for several months and being released, Buster Eason walked down the aisle of my church one Sunday morning in the middle of the service. Many of us had prayed so hard for so long for that day, and the people broke into loud applause and other expressions of joy.

Old Buster ... former hippie ... cocaine dealer ... fugitive from justice ... had sat around pot parties tearing down most institutions, including the church ... but that church had loved him, received him, prayed for him, visited him in prison, and welcomed him home.

As he came up on the platform, he whispered, "I've heard a lot about the institutional church, but today, I want to thank God for that institutional church."

Have you been to church lately?

You will be very welcome!

For I was an hungred, and ye gave
me meat: I was thirsty, and ye
gave me drink: I was a stranger, and ye
took me in: Naked, and ye clothed me:
I was sick, and ye visited me:
I was in prison, and ye came unto me.
—Matthew 25:35–36

A SILVER TRUMPET DREAM

As a sixth grader, I used to sit up on the balcony and listen to our high school band play. I wanted to play in that band more than I had ever wanted anything. The sparkling silver instruments made my eyes water with desire. *My dream became to have a horn.*

My family was too poor for me to have a horn, so when a man came to town telling how you could get a silver trumpet by paying $1.00 per week, I took him home with me. When he made his presentation, Dad went out of the room to cry alone. He wanted me to have it so badly, and he couldn't see how he could manage, but somehow he did.

I made the band after a while, and music gripped me in school. I attended Wake Forest College and became Band President. God gave me my first job in church ... because of that trumpet. Hey, friend, take time for a kid's dream... Jesus did!

And whoso shall receive one such little child in my name receiveth me.
—Matthew 18:5

DR. VANDER WARNER, JR.

WHAT TO DO UNTIL
THE WORLD ENDS

During the 1960 presidential campaign, John F. Kennedy concluded a very moving speech with the story of a judge in Hartford, Connecticut, who was presiding in court one morning during the 17th century when an eclipse of the sun occurred. The courtroom began to panic. The Judge rapped for order and said, "If this be the end of the world, let us at least be found doing our duty. Bring in the candles!"

It is a good idea to give some time to something worth doing even when the world is coming to an end.

There is a great verse in the Bible about that!

Therefore, my beloved brethren,
be ye stedfast, unmoveable, always
abounding in the work of the Lord,
forasmuch as ye know that your
labour is not in vain in the Lord.
—1 Corinthians 15:58

GOT A LIGHT?

On a dark night, a flashlight does very little about the whole expanse of darkness, but at least you can see where you are going, and you are all right as long as you walk in the light. Another way you can make it in the darkness is if someone takes you by the hand, and then you will both make it through the darkness.

If you have a light that you can shed on the subject of life … let it be seen.

Jesus said, "You are the light of the world." So, if you've got any light … take somebody you care for by the hand and shine and sing along with me …

This little light of mine, I'm going to let it shine …
This little light of mine, I'm going to let it shine …
This little light of mine, I'm going to let it shine …
Let it shine, let it shine, let it shine!

Let your light so shine before men,
that they may see your good works,
and glorify your Father
which is in Heaven.
—Matthew 5:16

SEEING WHAT IS OUT OF SIGHT

There was a lady who got her first look at the ocean at Virginia Beach. "I thought the ocean would look larger than it does," she complained.

You'll never see the ocean with your eyes, for it can only be seen with your mind. It's only when you see what is out of sight that you can perceive the true bigness of things.

So it was with Jesus of Nazareth. The world says, "We thought God would be more impressive than this!"

"He that hath seen me hath seen the Father," Jesus said. In seeing Jesus, you see God, yet those who lack spiritual imaginations are disappointed in Him ..."Is this not Joseph's son?"

Well, the point of this is:

You can't see everything you need to see with just your eyes. Open your mind, you don't want to miss God's great ocean of truth.

For we walk by faith,
not by sight.
—2 Corinthians 5:7

SINGLE SHORT CANDLE

A man and an angel stood looking at the world.

"The glacier is so cold and dark," said the man.

"But, there are lights … tiny sparks," the angel pointed out.

"But what are *those* against the night?" asked the man. "The lights are so few."

"The more room for yours," replied the angel.

"What is one light on all that black and bitter ice?" asked the man.

"What can all the darkness in the world do to one *light*?" asked the angel.

"But where is the fire?" cried the man. "For without the fire, I can light no candle!"

So the angel held out to him, all unexpecting, a burning coal from the altar of the Invisible, whereas the man lifted his short candle and set it, in fear and trembling, out upon the glacier.

Some who passed by, weary and cold to the marrow, were thereby lighted past one danger and were set forward with good cheer upon their journey to the coming dawn (chosen from *Candles on the Glacier*).

For thou wilt light my candle:
the Lord my God will
enlighten my darkness.
—Psalm 18:28

COMMUNICATE

While sitting outside my home in the woods, writing, I became aware of the scolding of a brace of little wrens. They were pretty afraid of me and were scolding me for being in their space.

Wrens are my favorite birds. I've rescued several of them from danger, fed them in the winter, and held their babies in my hand. I love those sassy little creatures, but they know nothing about how I feel about them. They stand off from me, look at me funny, and probably think wrong things about me.

It will never be any different because we can't communicate.

There are also some people standing off, a little scared, and scolding God or His church because they really don't know what is in His heart about them and how His church loves them.

That could be different if they would communicate with God and His people. They would then stop scolding and start singing.

But to do good and to communicate
forget not: for with such sacrifices
God is well pleased.
—Hebrews 13:16

THE SUPREME COURT JUSTICE AND DUCK HUNTING

I was ushered into the private chambers of United States Supreme Justice Lewis F. Powell, Jr., of Virginia after I had watched an awesome session of the Court.

As we conversed, I asked him if there was any particular area of federal law he had a special interest in and, if so, what it was.

He didn't hesitate a second. Flashing a broad smile, he said, "I'm interested in duck hunting!" That was quite refreshing. He was in his seventies and had a right not to work at all. He had learned the value of relaxing.

Jesus said, "Come apart and rest awhile" (Mark 6:31).

Someone else said, "All work and no play makes Jack a dull boy."

I'll tell you something else. "All work and no play makes Jack a dead boy."

Come alive. Play some today.

GIVE SOMEBODY A
GOLDEN APPLE TODAY

My dad's been dead for several years, but he was my chief encourager. I still miss him.

Years ago, on my twenty-fifth birthday, he sent me a telegram.

I've kept it in a safe place all these years. Let me share it with you:

"Happy Birthday, son. A few years ago, a gift from God was given to us. This gift has proven to be the son our hearts desired as a servant of our Lord."

It's about worn out now, but I get it every now and then and read it again.

The Bible says, "A word fitly spoken is like apples of gold in pictures of silver" (Proverbs 25:11).

That's what I mean by giving someone a golden apple today. They can't eat it, but it will strengthen them.

DADDY'S BOOK

One of the finest compliments ever paid me was by one of my daughters, who was four at the time.

It was the end of the Sunday morning service. I had gone to the door to greet people and nearly everyone was gone. She came toward me, holding up the Bible I had used earlier. Holding it out toward me, she said, "Daddy's Book, Daddy's Book!"

I haven't always lived up to that Book like I want to, but I'm glad that that wonderful little tyke had identified me with the Bible.

It was *my* mother and father's Book.

It's a great thing to imprint a child with the fact that when you turn for the answers to life's questions, you turn to the Bible.

If it really is your Book, that child will know it. They never miss a thing.

Seek ye out of the book of
the Lord, and read: ...
—Isaiah 34:16a

RETROSPECT

Here's a bit of verse from a man wistfully thinking of what happened to his childish dreams:

Over the hills and far away,
I see you, little lad at play,
With curly head and cheeks of tan,
A-dreaming, a-dreaming of the man,
The 'great big man' that you would be!
I wonder, dare I let you see,
Just what the years have done to me,
That little lad that used to be.

Most of us have had thoughts like that. That's why the words of Christ are so encouraging. He said you can begin again. He actually said, "You can be born anew from above."

You can be young—twice!

Marvel not that I said unto thee,
Ye must be born again.
—John 3:7

GETTING BACK YOUR DEAD

Two missionaries in Korea were transporting the dead body of their little eight-year-old girl to a burial site.

Two old Korean women couldn't help but overhear them in their mourning. After awhile, one of the women began to cry. Her companion asked why. The crying woman said, "I'm weeping for those two Americans who have lost their child."

The other responded, "Weep for yourself, old woman. Those Christians have a strange way of getting back their dead."

That's what every Sunday is about: the celebration of that truth.

The first and only person ever to be raised from the dead, never to die again.

Jesus said, "He that believeth in me, though he were dead, yet shall he live again?"
—(John 2:25b).

DR. VANDER WARNER, JR.

HELPING A KID WITH HIS TRICYCLE

When my church was in the inner-city, occasionally, I would walk along streets where many poor people lived. Once, when I was strolling along, I saw a little lad, a pre-schooler, struggling with his tricycle. He had a pair of pliers too big for his little hands and a loose nut he couldn't manage.

I offered a helping hand. It was easy for me to tighten the nut, thereby stabilizing his handlebars so he could guide his tricycle.

When I finished, I said, "Do you know who I am?"

He looked deeply into my eyes and said, "Jesus?"

"No, but I know Him, and He loves you," I managed to say.

Since then, I've often wished more people could see, in the things I do, the One who has done everything for me.

... Sir, we would see Jesus.
—John 12:21b

HAVING IT OUR WAY

I caught the words of a country song the other day that went something like this:

> *How can love survive,*
> *When we keep choosing sides?*
> *Who picks up the pieces,*
> *When two fools collide?*

Can you see that couple asserting their rights, trying to have his or her way, running into each other's desires, feelings, and expectations?

The Bible said something about two becoming one.

I think we've worn ourselves out exploring individuality and separateness. We aren't going to make it in marriage until we discover one-ness!

And said, For this cause shall a man leave father and mother, and shall cleave to his wife: and they twain shall be one flesh? Wherefore they are no more twain, but one flesh. What therefore God hath joined together, let not man put asunder.
—Matthew 19:5–6

BE AN ANGEL

My good friend Dick Hemby, an exciting radio personality and a man struggling with his faith, said to me, "If God would just send a little angel to stand there on my coffee table and say, 'Richard, I have a message from God. He says, 'I love you.'' Then, if the angel could put an indelible mark on my arm so afterward I'd know I wasn't dreaming, I could believe better."

I shared that on my television program.

Later that week, a lovely voice on the telephone to Dick said, "Mr. Hemby, this is your angel. I just wanted you to know that God loves you. Goodbye."

I've thought about that a lot.

I'm not very angelic, and perhaps you don't see yourself in that light either. We all fall pretty far short of angelic goodness; *however*, you'll like this ...

The next best thing to being an angel is to act like one. Go ahead and tell somebody that God loves them.

For He shall give his angels
charge over thee, to keep
thee in all thy ways.
—Psalm 91:11

WHERE IS HAPPINESS?

Where is happiness?

NOT IN MONEY—Jay Gould, the American millionaire philosopher, had plenty of that. When dying, he said, "I suppose I'm the most miserable man on earth."

NOT IN POSITION AND FAME—Lord Beaconsfield enjoyed more than his share of both. He wrote, "Youth is a mistake, manhood a struggle, old age a regret ..."

NOT IN PLEASURE—Lord Byron lived a life of pleasure if anyone ever did, yet at age twenty-eight, he wrote, "The worm, the canker and grief are mine alone."

NOT IN DISBLIEF—Voltaire was an infidel of the most pronounced type. He wrote, "I wish I had never been born."

WHERE IS HAPPINESS?—In Christ alone! Christ said, "I will see you again, and your heart shall rejoice and your joy no man takes from you" (John 16:22).

Be happy ... be Christian.

LIFE WORTH LIVING?

What makes life worth living? Here are some lines that might help with that question:

> *What makes life worth the living*
> *Is our giving and forgiving.*
> *Giving tiny bits of kindness*
> *That will leave a joy behind us*
> *And forgiving bitter trifles*
> *That the right word often stifles,*
> *For the little things are bigger*
> *Than we often stop to figure.*
> *What makes life worth the living*
> *Is our giving and forgiving!*

Paul the Apostle put it beautifully and practically when he said ...

> ***Forbearing one another, and***
> ***forgiving one another, if any man***
> ***have a quarrel against any:***
> ***even as Christ forgave you,***
> ***so also do ye.***
> ***—Colossians 3:13***

ENCOURAGEMENT FOR LIVING

Not too long ago, in Richmond, Virginia, a teenager, after an argument with his girlfriend, drove up to a hill overlooking a deepwater terminal. His bright lights pierced the darkness above the water. He stopped for a full minute and then accelerated his car off the embankment into fifty feet of water.

I wonder what went through his troubled, anxious mind just before he accelerated? I wonder what were his thoughts and prayers of that minute?

What could you or I have said that might have stopped him? What torment was he experiencing that drove him to give up on life?

He's gone, but my question is, "Is there anybody in my life or yours who needs a word from us that might free them to want to live?"

The Bible says, "Encourage one another" (1 Thessalonians 5:11).

DR. VANDER WARNER, JR.

WHERE ARE YOU SAFE?

In Florida, a gunman entered the correctional center in Pompano Beach and robbed an inmate of a TV, stereo, and radio. The inmate was serving a sentence for armed robbery. "If you're not safe in prison," said Superintendent Barry Ahringer, "where are you safe?"

Talk about the ironic!

It reminds me of a statement by Saint Peter, "Be thoughtful, very alert, because your adversary the devil, like a roaring lion, prowls about seeking whom he may devour" (1 Peter 5:8–9).

Saint Peter goes on to say, "Resist him stedfastly in the faith ..."

That answers Superintendent Ahringer's question, "Where are you safe?" — in the faith!

If you are a person of faith,
You are in an impregnable fortress,
And Satan can huff and puff,
But never blow your house down!

Be sober, be vigilant; because your
adversary the devil, as a roaring lion,
walketh about, seeking whom he may devour:
Whom resist stedfast in the faith, knowing
that the same afflictions are accomplished
in your brethren that are in the world.
—1 Peter 5:8–9

WHEN WE FLY AGAIN

As I walked outside my home, a baby wren was startled and flew into one of our plate glass windows. Several birds have done that and broken their necks against the window of our home here in the country.

The little bird bounced off back to the ground and was buried in the leaves. My heart sank—not my favorite little bird!

I went over and stroked her feathers. She didn't move, but she seemed to blink very slowly. I went to get my wife so she could see the fascinating little creature up close.

My thoughts were, "Surely God must be sad when we do ourselves in because we mistake the events of life and fly into disaster. He feels about us like I feel about this little bird."

Mrs. Warner came out, picked the bird up, and exclaimed over its delicate bill and beautiful feathers.

With an annoyed little scolding chirp, the baby wren flew away. What joy surged in both our hearts and in God's too when we fly again!

I have no greater joy than to hear
that my children walk in truth.
—3 John 1:4

DR. VANDER WARNER, JR.

WAIT TILL YOU GET
CLOSE ENOUGH TO JUDGE

I was speaking to a congregation in Baltimore, Maryland, to whom I had never spoken before.

As I warmed to my presentation, I noticed a couple with their heads down, not looking at me. That really began to bother me more and more. I inserted a few comments about people who didn't care about the Bible and spiritual things. I made a few other attempts to get their attention, to no avail, and finally proceeded with a little burn going on inside me.

After the service, the couple was brought to me by their friend and introduced. It was then that I discovered … they were blind!

They weren't looking off, they weren't looking anywhere.

That's been a smart little reminder to me to avoid judging people until I've been up close to them.

As it says in the Bible, "… understand one another" (1 Peter 3:7a, ESV).

FLOP PROOF

One of the greatest of all, the Billy Graham Crusades, took place in Madison Square Garden in New York City.

Mrs. Warner and I saw Ethel Waters, the great black entertainer, in the choir. She never missed a night of the crusade.

When she was interviewed by the press, she was asked, "Do you think the Crusade will be a success?"

She responded with a classic comment, "Yes, God doesn't sponsor no flops!"

I love that. I need to remember that.

If you've been failing, maybe you need a new sponsor, the One that doesn't sponsor "no flops!"

We sing about that often in my church, "Nothing is impossible with God."

How to be flop-proof? Make God your sponsor!

For with God nothing
shall be impossible.
—Luke 1:37

PRAYER HELPS YOU TALK BETTER

Did you hear the story about the two parrots?

One was owned by a deacon, and it could say, "Let's hug and kiss."

The other was owned by a minister, and it could only say, "Let's pray."

The deacon and minister decided to get them together so they might learn from each other and expand their vocabularies.

As the deacon's parrot was put into the cage with the minister's parrot, it said, "Let's hug and kiss."

The minister's parrot said, "Praise the Lord, my prayers have been answered."

Some wonderful things may be waiting on your learning to pray.

The Bible says, "Ye have not because ye ask not" (James 4:2a).

Oh, there's more to it than that, but not less than that.

NO LOSE FIGHTS AT HOME

Do you remember the trial of General William Westmoreland and CBS? Both sides claimed victory.

Do you remember the trial with the Israeli Prime Minister and Time magazine? Both sides claimed victory.

I didn't follow those two trials closely enough to know the details, but that is a very desirable outcome.

In a fight with your friend or your spouse, the only fight worth fighting is one in which both gain something at the end, a fight in which both sides win victory. A one-sided victory in the home is no victory.

It's not a matter of letting him or her win but of letting us win! See to it, no matter what, that your spouse is a winner.

There's a Bible verse that goes like this:

See that no one repays another with
evil for evil, but always seek that
which is good for one another
and for all people.
—1 Thessalonians 5:15 (AMP)

DR. VANDER WARNER, JR.

COMING BACK GOD'S WAY

The story is told of a widow who raised one son, sent him to Cambridge, and later saw him off to the service of his country. His death in active service was a crushing blow. One night, she dreamed that an angel came and offered her the privilege of having her son back for five minutes at any stage of his life.

She decided not to ask for him as a college student or as a man among men, but as the disobedient boy who ran out into the garden angry, only to return and throw himself sobbing into her arms in repentance.

This is the way God wants us, and it is the only way we can come from our way to His way!

The Lord is not slack concerning his promise, as some men count slackness, but is longsuffering to usward, not willing that any should perish, but that all should come to repentance.
—2 Peter 3:9

NO SEPARATION, NO WAY

George Locke, a sailor lad in World War II, wrote home these deep words of faith:

"If you should hear that I have fallen, do not weep. Remember, the deepest ocean in which my body sinks in death is only a pool in the hand of my Saviour."

That's what the great Negro Spiritual means:

> "He's got the whole world in His hands,
> He's got the whole world in His hands."

The verse that I like best says:

> "He's got YOU and ME, brother, in His hands,
> He's got the whole world in His hands."

And for the believer, that is what the resurrection of Easter is all about. The Apostle Paul wrote:

For I am persuaded that neither death, nor life, nor angels, nor principalities, nor powers, nor things present, nor things to come, Nor height, nor depth, nor any other creature, shall be able to separate us from the love of God, which is in Christ Jesus our Lord.
—Romans 8:38–39

WHERE IS GRANDDADDY?

The little six-year-old stood at the casket in which lay the body of his granddaddy.

As he watched the people come by crying, he couldn't figure it out, and so finally, he asked his mother, "Mommy, where did you tell me Granddaddy was?"

She replied, "With Jesus in heaven."

"Well, Mommy, if Granddaddy is in heaven with Jesus, why is everybody crying?"

Well, there is more to it than that, of course. It is tough for family and friends to say goodbye for even a little while, but the ringing truth is that when believers die, they go somewhere. Believers go somewhere worth going to. Death is not a dead end!

That is one reason we go to church on Easter and every other Sunday, actually. We go to celebrate the victory of life over death, and we go to say, "Thanks be to God that giveth us the victory through Jesus Christ!" (1 Corinthians 15:57).

We are confident, I say, and willing rather to be absent from the body, and to be present with the Lord.
—2 Corinthians 5:8

WHAT'S WORSE THAN HAVING NO VOICE?

Dr. William E. Sangster, a popular preacher at Westminister, Central Hall, London, held fast to a deep evangelical faith. A year or two before his death, he contracted an illness that slowly robbed him of his power of speech. His son, Paul, wrote in his biography, "I heard him preach the most wonderful sermons I've ever heard in my life, but I never heard him preach like he did the last three months of his life when he couldn't whisper a word. It was beautiful to see his lovely, radiant, peaceful, trusting life when he was running to the end."

On his last Easter morning, he wrote to his daughter, who was a missionary in India, "Margaret, what a dreadful thing to wake up on Easter morning and have no voice with which to shout, 'He is risen,' but how far more awful to have a voice and not want to shout it."

I just thought of something worse: having a voice with nothing to shout about.

I have fought a good fight,
I have finished my course,
I have kept the faith.
—2 Timothy 4:7

ON GOD AND STONES

A young man struggling with his faith, especially about the resurrection of Jesus and life after death, questioned my friend, Dr. Robert G. Lee. He was puzzled as to how Jesus could have moved the massive stone that sealed the tomb.

Dr. Lee said, "Son, have you ever heard of a neutrino? It's a particle or wave of light that can travel through one mile of solid lead. If God could make something that could go through a mile of solid lead, surely He could go through a crack in a rock!"

I love it! But the truth is, God didn't remove the stone so Jesus could get out, but so people could get in to see that Jesus was gone.

He is not here; for he is risen, as he said. Come, see the place where the Lord lay.
—Matthew 28:6

SUNDAY'S COMING!

There is a great black preacher in Philadelphia who has an Easter sermon called "Sunday's Coming." Sunday and Resurrection are synonymous in his sermon.

He talks about what's happening on Friday ... the Friday Jesus is crucified ... they capture Him ... He's being convicted ... they're beating Him ... but SUNDAY'S COMING!

They nail Him to the Cross ... between thieves and He's thirsty ... but SUNDAY'S COMING!

Everybody forsakes Him ... the sky turns black ... God the Father turns His back and Jesus cries out in intolerable loneliness ... but SUNDAY'S COMING!

He dies, they put Him in a tomb and close the entrance with a massive stone and say, "That's that"... but SUNDAY'S COMING!

This may be an awful day in your life ... but SUNDAY'S COMING!

Blessed be the God and Father of our Lord Jesus Christ, which according to his abundant mercy hath begotten us again unto a lively hope by the resurrection of Jesus Christ from the dead.
—1 Peter 1:3

PRAYER ABOUT "THINGS" OR ME

I collect prayers, and I got one a little while ago that's prayable for all of us.

It goes like this:

"Lord, if you won't change things for me, change me for things."

Here is a thought that is good enough for everyone to think about:

"Not this thing, nor that thing, but me, Oh, Lord, standing in need of prayer!"

Hear my prayer, O God;
give ear to the words
of my mouth.
—Psalm 54:2

WHO'S TO SAY
WHO'S TO BLAME

It's easy to slip into blaming others for our own faults, like the country preacher who was learning new words, and in the middle of a sermon, he shouted, "It's propaganda."

He questioned his wife to see if she noticed the big word. She had! Did he ask her if she knew what the word meant? He didn't!

She said, "Well, in my marriage to Bill, we had three children; in my marriage to Tom, we had two children; but in my marriage to you, we've had none; so, it looks to me like I'm the right goose but you ain't the 'proper gander.'"

I just had to share that bit of humor with you, but it's not stretching the truth too much to say that Jesus was talking about that when He said, "If you've got a log in your own eye, don't criticize somebody else who has just a chip" (Matthew 7:3).

You ain't the "proper gander" to criticize!

OF BEGGARS AND BREAD

Lee Iacocca was on the front of Time magazine, and the caption with the photograph was a quote from Iacocca, "I gotta tell you." That's the man … confident, successful, with something he's "gotta tell you."

It reminded me of a time when I went to share my faith with a young adult who grew madder by the minute. When I finished, he said, "I don't need no preacher coming out here, sitting on his throne, telling me about God."

I said, "Bob, I'm sorry I came across that way. What I was trying to say is that if we were both beggars and I found bread, I'd tell you about the bread and share it with you. Bob, I am a beggar, and I have found the 'Bread of Life' … and as one beggar to another, I want you to have some."

And two beggars knelt side by side,
And Bob the beggar took the bread,
And thanked the Bread Giver.

For the bread of God is he which
cometh down from heaven, and
giveth life unto the world.
—John 6:33

WHEN SCRATCHING FOR IT WON'T HELP

We have a bird feeder out in "Greater Short Pump," where I live in the woods, but the birds haven't found it yet.

When it snowed, they came around scratching under the edge of the house while just over their heads was enough food to feed a flock of birds. They were hungry and frightened, flitting here and there. Frightened, but not knowing what to be afraid of. If they would just look up!

When we all get to heaven one great day, one of the greatest surprises of all, I believe, will be to learn about all the good things we've missed because we didn't look up and ask for them.

Jesus said, "Fear not little flock, it is your Father's pleasure to give you the Kingdom" (Luke 12:32).

DR. VANDER WARNER, JR.

EATING BY GRACE

One of my favorite places to eat in Richmond is O'Brienstein's. They serve fresh, hot bagels with whipped butter while you wait for your meal, then have a fresh and varied salad bar and the best quiche in town!

Mrs. Warner and I go there often for lunch since it is near my office. Once in a while, when it's time to get our check, the waiter will say, with a twinkle, "Your meal has been taken care of," and then he gives me the name of a member of my church.

Now, that's a nice experience—excellent food and the bill paid for by a friend. That's what you call *eating by grace.*

The Bible talks about being saved by grace. What that means is you get a reservation in heaven, and God pays the bill!

That in the ages to come he might shew the exceeding riches of his grace in his kindness toward us through Christ Jesus.
—Ephesians 2:7

JUMP WITH ALL YOUR HEART

Faith has been defined by using each letter of the word as an acrostic:

F–orsaking
A–ll
I
T–ake
H–im

Another person said believing is a leap of faith. Believing does require more of the heart than the head. There will always be some things left to be understood later, always!

We are like the track star who was a high jumper. The coach put the bar to the highest possible notch. The jumper looked at it and said, "Coach, how can I ever jump that high?"

"I'll tell you how," replied the coach, "just throw your heart over that bar first, and the rest is sure to follow."

The Good Book puts it, "You'll find him if you seek him with all your heart" (Deuteronomy 4:29).

STRANGE THING ABOUT JESUS

I love studying the Gospels. You can find Jesus showing up in the strangest places and with the strangest people. One of the things that "bugged" the religious organizations of His day was that He was always around sinners. They said, "He eats with sinners."

They could never get it through their heads that Jesus loved sinful, even outcast people, but I've discovered Jesus majored in sinful people.

Many of the religious people kept trying to convince Him of their goodness and righteousness. They kept missing who He was and the whole point of His coming. Jesus said, "The righteous don't need me. I've come to seek and save the lost."

I see it pretty clearly now. When I admit the worst things about me, that's when I'm getting ready to experience the best thing that ever happened to me—FORGIVENESS!

For the Son of Man is come
to save that which was lost.
—Matthew 18:11

LOOK UP ... AND REST

Corrie Ten Boom was the grand old lady of Amsterdam. Her father died in a German jail where he was sent for helping the Jews escape the Nazis. Corrie watched her sister die in a prisoner-of-war camp from overwork.

Corrie became what she called "God's tramp." She went everywhere telling how you could still love in the midst of great hatred and how you could survive when everything you could see was against you.

One time, she put one of her secrets of survival this way: "When I look in, I'm depressed. When I look around, I'm depressed. When I look up, *I'm at rest.*"

The Psalmist said, "I will lift up mine eyes unto the hills, from whence cometh my help" (Psalm 121:1).

My help comes from the Lord. Look up and rest!

DR. VANDER WARNER, JR.

THE ATMOSPHERE OF A GOOD MEAL

One of my favorite places to eat is the Williamsburg Inn in Colonial Williamsburg, Virginia. It costs more than a nickel, so I can't go often, but it is always a joy. Why? Atmosphere, waiters hovering over you bringing bread, relishes and food, the crisp tablecloths, music by a harpist, the silver service, and candles—it's the atmosphere for a wonderful meal.

But I'll tell you something. It's no better than the first meal my wife ever cooked for me at our "little bitty mobile home" on the campus of Wake Forest University while we were students there.

The explanation is a Bible verse in Proverbs, "A dinner of vegetables with love is better than the finest beef and hatred with it" (Proverbs 15:16).

So the atmosphere for a good meal is love! Sometimes, it's costly to love, but the atmosphere is worth the extra. Not only the food, but life itself tastes better.

THE DANGER OF INCONSIDERATION

Dr. Morris Ashcraft, in one of his books, tells about his oldest brother, who was killed one night in a head-on collision that could have been avoided.

It was raining and dark on a narrow road, and the truck had no red or yellow running lights on the edges of the large body.

The young man pulled over as far as he thought necessary, but the sides of the truck, invisible in the darkness, stuck out far beyond the cab. That part of the truck ripped into the sides and top of the car and killed him as the truck passed.

His last words just before the impact were, "He won't dim his lights."

A lack of consideration of our fellow man may not kill them, but it puts them down so that it really hurts. God's Book of Loving Principles says very simply, "Consider one another" (Hebrews 10:24).

REMEMBER WHO IS
BACKING YOU

The worst job I ever had—the very worst—was selling Bibles for Southwestern Distributors during the summer of my freshman year in college. One of the worst places I ever tried to sell Bibles was in Myrtle Beach, South Carolina. It got so bad that I didn't even have money for food.

At that point, the sales manager had a pep meeting. He reviewed sales techniques, closing techniques and finally, after glancing at me, said, "Don't be worried and don't be blue. Southwestern Distributors is backing you."

It sounded exciting at the time, and so I gave it another whirl. I have revised that encouraging thought to read:

"Don't be worried and don't be blue, God the Father is backing you!"

Yes, that's in the Bible, "If God be for us, who can be against us?" (Romans 8:31).

PURPOSE HAS
LIFE-GIVING POWER

Viktor Frankl, a Jewish psychiatrist incarcerated in a concentration camp during World War II, learned the power of purpose. He noticed that those people who had a strong reason for living could endure more and live longer, while those with less reason for living gave up more quickly and died.

He survived it all because each morning, he looked for something to do during the day that would help someone else. By doing that, he found a reason for living.

He developed a whole new method of psychotherapy based on this discovery. He wrote that a person could survive almost any WHAT in life if that person had a real WHY for living.

For Jesus and those who follow Him, the "WHY" is the will of God. What a motivation!

And Jesus said, "Inasmuch as ye have done it unto the least of these, you have done it unto me" (Matthew 25:40).

You've got something worth living for as long as you've got somebody to help.

DR. VANDER WARNER, JR.

DON'T EAT WITH THE CHICKENS

The great Danish philosopher Soren Kierkegaard tells the parable of the wild goose who stopped in the barnyard for food on his way north.

The pickings were so easy he stayed another day. On the third day, a flock of wild geese flew over and honked at him. He looked up, thought about taking off with them, but thought about the easy food and went on eating with the ducks and chickens.

The next day, another flock of his brothers flew over, and he looked up again, but no. And on the fifth day, when they flew over and honked at him, he didn't even look up ...!

You and I were made for better things than living life at the lowest possible level.

The Bible is really clear that we were made for God.

Of course, if you want to soar to the heights, there will be a lot of turkeys trying to hold you back, but chicken feed ain't worth it!

I will ascend above the heights of
the clouds; I will be like the most High.
—Isaiah 14:14

YOU CAN MAKE IT TODAY

Robert Louis Stevenson said, "Anyone can carry his burden, however heavy, until nightfall. Anyone can do his work, however hard, for one day. Anyone can live sweetly, patiently, lovingly, purely, 'til the sun goes down, and this is all that life really means."

I agree and disagree with Stevenson; sometimes that's all there is to life for that day—toughing it out till night because tomorrow is another day, and I'll manage tomorrow when it gets here.

That's what Jesus meant when He said, "Each day has enough evil in it for that day." So, take life one day at a time.

The Bible says that God will provide whatever you need for this day. Yesterday is gone, tomorrow is not here, and you and God can make it today!

But my God shall supply all your need according to his riches in glory by Christ Jesus.
—Philippians 4:19

ONE MORE ROUND!

James J. Corbett, former heavyweight champion of the world, an athlete with limited physical equipment but with great competitive spirit, said, "Fight one more round. When your feet are so tired that you have to shuffle back to the center of the ring, fight one more round. When your arms are so tired that you can hardly lift your hands to come on guard, fight one more round. When your nose is bleeding and your eyes are black and blue and you are so tired that you wish your opponent would crack you on the jaw and put you to sleep ... don't quit ... fight one more round!"

Don't quit yet! Fight!

One more round! Just one more ...! One ...!

Won!

I have fought a good fight,
I have finished my course,
I have kept the faith...
—2 Timothy 4:7

100+ ONE-MINUTE THOUGHT MANAGERS

HOW TO SETTLE YOUR STOMACH

It's been estimated that in one lifetime, the average citizen will consume 150 head of cattle, 2400 chickens, 226 lambs, 26 sheep, 310 pigs, 26 acres of grain, and 50 acres of fruit and vegetables. That's a lot of food.

In his book about the Bible, John MacArthur asked, "But how much are we consuming of the Word of God, which gives us eternal life?"

An outdoor bulletin board at a church in Quincy, Massachusetts, carried the message, "A Bible that is falling apart usually belongs to someone who isn't."

When the stuff of life makes you a bit sick, refresh yourself with the milk of the Word. It will settle your stomach and your life.

As newborn babes, desire the
sincere milk of the Word,
that ye may grow thereby.
—1 Peter 2:2

GRACIOUS GLANDS

"We've all wished, at one time or another, that we could reach back to a painful moment and cut it out of our lives. Some people are fortunate and seem to have gracious glands that secrete the juices of forgetfulness and forgiveness. These people never hold a grudge. They do not remember old hurts, and their painful yesterdays die with the coming of tomorrows. However, most people find that the pains of the past keep rolling through our memories, and there is nothing we can do to stop the flow." (This excerpt is from Charles Swindoll's *The Seasons of Life.*)

Hannah Arendt, in her book *The Human Condition,* shared her discovery of the only power that can stop the flowing stream of painful memories—the "faculty of forgiveness." That is a simple message, but oh, so hard.

Here is help: "Father, forgive us as we forgive one another. In Jesus' name."

For if ye forgive men their trespasses,
your heavenly Father will
also forgive you.
—Matthew 6:14

WHEN FORGIVENESS IS REAL

From the striking book *Forgive and Forget* by Lewis Snedes is this:

"Myra is a beautiful woman, an actress, who was almost killed by a hit-and-run driver a few years ago. Her husband, a TV and film star, stayed with her only until she recovered from the accident. Then, coldly and quickly, he took off and left her alone in her wheelchair."

I asked Myra if she had been able to forgive him.

She said, "I think so."

"Why?"

"Well, I find myself wishing him well."

I bore down. "Suppose you learned that he had married a sexy starlet. Could you pray for his happiness?"

"Yes, I could, and I would. Steve needs love very much, and I want him to have it."

What peace!

You will know that forgiveness has begun when you recall those who hurt you and feel the power to wish them well!

Be not overcome of evil, but
overcome evil with good.
—Romans 12:21

DR. VANDER WARNER, JR.

ANOTHER VOICE TO HEAR FROM

My friend, Harvey Hudson, the popular radio personality in Richmond, is a pretty earthy fellow, but he's not stupid. He knows that God is a reality to be reckoned with.

Often, he uses a verse from the Bible on the air, usually from the Old Testament, and he reads it without comment.

I think he is saying that in the midst of a tough world or a tough day, there is another who ought to be heard from, and He speaks to us through the Bible.

Somebody is trying to get through to you. Somebody, the only "body" who really knows what is going on, and He's quietly trying to get your attention.

If you've got time to pray—God's got time to listen.

He that hath ears
to hear, let him hear.
—Matthew 11:15

LEARN TO SHIFT TO A PLAY MODE

My dear dad was a diligent, hard-working, "long-houred" man, and it rubbed off. I have to work at not working. It generally makes me nervous to relax, but I really like it when finally I shift into a play mode.

The Bible says there is a time to work and a time to play. It's probably way past your play time, my friend!

Here's a little bit of verse that's worth trying to remember:

> *If you hold your nose to the grindstone rough*
> *And hold it down there long enough,*
> *You soon will say there is no such thing*
> *As a brook that babbles or a bird that sings.*
> *These three will all your world compose,*
> *Just you, the stone, and your ground-down nose.*

GIVE GOD HIGH VISIBILITY

Helen Keller, the brilliant deaf and blind mute, was being offered an honorary doctorate by a major university. She said, "I'll accept it if you give my teacher, Anne Sullivan, one too." Anne Sullivan had opened Helen's mind to God's beautiful world.

At the ceremony, when Anne Sullivan was honored, Miss Keller stood beside her and said, "She made me see the stars, the flowers, the world, but most of all, she made me see God!"

That's what old-time Christians mean when they talk about glorifying God. To glorify God means to make Him visible and give Him high visibility. That's heavy!

Today, you can help somebody see!

We always carry around in our body the death of Jesus, so that the life of Jesus may also be revealed in our body.
—2 Corinthians 4:10 (NIV)

BLOOD ON THE FILE

Jesus said a remarkably thrilling thing: Not one tiny character of His Father's Word would be destroyed. It's called the indestructible Word. God's Word gets easier to believe all the time. Every conceivable device has been used against the Bible, but it "keeps beating its enemies back from the grave."

It reminds me of something I read about the devil and the Bible. The devil is a serpent; the Bible is a file, and the serpent attacks the file ferociously. He gnaws away with his serpent's teeth against the file. He gnaws and gnaws and is certain that he's wearing the file away until, one day, he notices blood on the file.

When we really take a look, it's exciting to discover that Jesus knew what he was talking about!

For verily I say unto you,
Till heaven and earth pass, one jot
or one tittle shall in no wise pass
from the law, till all be fulfilled.
—Matthew 5:18

BREAKING A FALSEHOOD CYCLE

Jess Duboy, Richmond, Virginia's very successful advertising executive, is quite a man. You've seen him all across the nation selling cars. Jess is a winner and has been from a child. He achieved some fame, made a lot of money, had a prestigious address, and drove those cars that made you look twice. The best thing Jess Duboy did was marry a former Miss Virginia, who was a godly woman.

Jess was an agnostic, and his dad was an atheist, but to please his wife, Jess went to church for fifteen years and listened. He kept telling himself the wrong things. Good things kept blocking out the main thing because he was in a thought cycle of falsehood. I call it his "ignorance cycle."

That beautiful, brainy wife *kept him in the presence of truth,* and one day, it broke down that wrong cycle.

Now he really is successful … and he can sleep at night.

---

*Come unto me, all ye that labour
and are heavy laden,
and I will give you rest.*
—Matthew 11:28

LIFE-SAVING LAUGH

Here is one about laughing your head on. If this is a lie, E. Stanley Jones told it. During the Communist takeover in China, a missionary was being led to a place of execution where her head was going to be chopped off as they had done to others.

Going down the hill with her captors, she started laughing out loud. The soldiers got angry and asked her what she was laughing at. She said, "I'm laughing at what my head will look like rolling down the hill while I go up to heaven to be with Jesus."

They said, "Well, if it makes you happy, we won't kill you," and they didn't!

That's laughing your head on, or is it laughing yourself to life?

You're saying no way! You're right—unless ulcers count too. Treat yourself and someone else to a laugh for life!

A merry heart doeth good like a medicine: but a broken spirit drieth the bones.
—Proverbs 17:22

DR. VANDER WARNER, JR.

A WAY INTO THE
PRESENCE OF KINGS

My friend, Hatcher Story, of Courtland, Virginia, is a remarkable character. The newspapers call him the "entrepreneur peanut farmer." Those peanuts are magic. I went with him to Sardi's—yes, the real Sardi's in New York where the stars go.

The maitre d' at Sardi's came over, smiled, and said, "Yes, Sir, Mr. Story." The first thing Hatcher did was hand him a couple of pounds of the world's most delicious parched peanuts. How can you feel anything but warm toward a guy who gives you peanuts?

I met several Broadway stars on that trip. They were just as glad to see Hatcher as he was to see them.

Hatcher sends those peanuts, and sometimes country hams, to a lot of people. It's no wonder that some of the outstanding people in America have been to his doorstep.

Peanuts? Nah! They could buy them, but these were a gift!

A man's gift maketh room for him,
and bringeth him before great men.
—Proverbs 18:16

Thanks be unto God for
his unspeakable gift.
—2 Corinthians 9:15

TAKE A MINUTE FOR YOURSELF

The best thing you can do for everybody you love is to love yourself. The idea has been around for a long time, but we are just learning how crucial it is.

I had not seen the idea articulated in more practical terms than in the little book *Take a Minute for Yourself.*

The thesis for the book is this: The best thing you can do for yourself is to love yourself. The best experience is to be loved and the best way to be loved is to love, and the best way to get love is to give it.

One more step: The best way to give love is to do something the other person wants you to do.

So, the best thing you can do for yourself is to take a minute for yourself by taking a minute for someone else. Before it's all over, they will give it right back to you.

And not only that ... it will feel good going and coming.

Here's a verse with a strange twist that fits right here:

"Not because I desire a gift; but I desire fruit that may abound to your account" (Philippians 4:17).

HOW TO HANDLE TEARS

"Tears need an arm around the shoulder, not some sage piece of advice or stern lecture." I give Charles Stanley credit for that. I think it's in his book, *Is There a Man in the House.*

Remember the time(s) your daughter tearfully told you about losing a boyfriend, and wise, old, comforting dad would respond with a "Now ... now ... there are plenty of fish in the sea."

How shocking that she didn't seem helped at all. Indeed, she probably pulled away and went to her room. Why? You were trying to get her to feel like you. No way! The Bible teaches us the opposite, i.e., we are to match our emotions to theirs.

Paul puts it, "Rejoice with them that rejoice, (but when they lose a boyfriend) weep with them that weep." And don't mix those emotions! When you don't know what to say, Dad, don't say it. Put your arm around her shoulder.

That's enough for right now. There will be another day to talk about fish.

Rejoice with them that do rejoice, and weep with them that weep.
—Romans 12:15

RELATIONSHIPS AND DISAGREEMENTS

"Dear, can't our relationship stand a disagreement?"

So said my wife to me while I was making a federal case out of a little conflict. It was one of those times, as I said in my Foreword, when "the nickel dropped."

The point was not that we weren't going to have any more disagreements. (When couples say they have never had a disagreement, I wonder which of them is lying or stupid?)

You see, I was lecturing my wife on how terrible it was for us to have a disagreement at all. She was saying that the disagreement is not so bad unless our relationship is riding on it. She was right!

I wasn't going to leave her because she wanted the thermostat at 60° and I wanted it at 70°. We just have more fires in the fireplace. We both like that.

Good marriages are not those that never have problems, but rather, good marriages deal with the problems when they arise.

Remember this old verse your mother used to give you: "Let not the sun go down on your wrath" (Ephesians 4:26b).

STRIKE A BLOW AGAINST EVIL

In my collection of prayers is this one prayed by Jack Taylor in my church a while ago:

"Lord, change my mind on every issue on which You and I don't see eye to eye."

R. Arthur Matthews in *Born for Battle* suggests that the greatest and most pivotal spiritual battle was waged by Jesus, not on the Cross of Calvary but in the Garden of Gethsemane. He reckons that Jesus, "wrestling" in prayer until perspiration became blood and bringing His will decisively in line with the Father's, was the place of real victory. He points out that Jesus, "on the road to the Cross," is seen as passive, a man acted upon, not a man active ... the Lamb of God ... a victim; but "in the quiet solitude of Gethsemane's olive grove, Jesus appears in an active role."

Life's greatest battles are in the arena of the will. Jack Taylor's prayer is my prayer too. It's a "Jesus-like" prayer.

It's the mightiest blow you can strike against evil, worldwide or heart-wide.

"I come against you, Satan ...

Thy will be one on earth (in my life)

As it is in heaven."

NEUTRALITY AND HELL

"There's a special place reserved in hell for those who, in a moment of crises, remain neutral" (Dante).

No man can serve two masters.

---

*"For either he will hate the one,
and love the other; or else he will hold
to the one and despise the other"
(Jesus in Matthew 6:24).*

Printed in the USA
CPSIA information can be obtained
at www.ICGtesting.com
LVHW011345140924
790865LV00014B/675